Baby and Beyond

Progression in Play for Babies and Children

Messy Play

Baby and Beyond - Messy Play

ISBN 1 905019 58 0

© Featherstone Education Ltd, 2006

Text © Sally Featherstone and Liz Williams, 2006; Illustrations © Martha Hardy, 2006; Series Editor, Sally Featherstone

First published in the UK, March 2006

'Baby and Beyond' is a trade mark of Featherstone Education Ltd

Published in the United Kingdom by

Featherstone Education Ltd, 44 - 46 High Street, Husbands Bosworth, Leicestershire, LE17 6LP

Printed in the UK on paper produced in the European Union from managed, sustainable forests

Contents

Baby and Beyond

A series of books for practitioners working with children from Birth to Three and beyond

This book gives ideas for introducing and extending tactile, explorative and messy play experiences for babies and young children. Each page spread contains a range of experiences and a selection of ideas for each of the four developmental stages of the Birth to Three Matters Framework, and extends this progression into the early Stepping Stones for the Foundation Stage:

Young Babies -
Heads Up, Lookers and Communicators
0-8 months

Babies -
Sitters, Standers and Explorers
8-18 months

Young Children -
Movers, Shakers and Players
18-24 months

Children -
Walkers, Talkers and Pretenders
24-36 months

Foundation Stage -
Yellow Stepping Stone and beyond
Foundation 1 and 2

Introduction

Messy play is an essential element of all Early Years settings. The experiences help babies and children to develop eye and hand control, fine motor skills, muscles and language. As children grow older, messy play gives a firm foundation to the use of tools and investigation of materials, extending their knowledge and understanding of the world around them. The activities described in this book are all appropriate to children from birth to five (and beyond) and we have linked them to the developmental stages of the curriculum guidance for Birth to Three and the Foundation Stage (soon to become the Early Years Foundation Stage).

Babies and children also need the company and stimulation of knowledgeable and interested adults if they are to extend their play into thinking and learning. Adult/child interaction is essential at all levels to encourage children's language, learning and development. Talking with and listening to babies and children is also vital in supporting and developing self-esteem. Observing their play is essential for recognising both their achievements and their needs, so you can plan for future learning.

As babies and children move through the developmental stages, experiences can be offered in differing ways and at different working heights - lying down, sitting (both propped and independent), kneeling or standing - and some children will develop preferences. Some older children will still enjoy working lying down, while some very young children will be determined to sit or stand even before they are able to do it alone! Using small and large trays (such as plant and builders' trays) are simple but effective ways to enable easy access for all babies and children. Young babies need to have access to the experiences at floor level, on an adult's knee and in their arms, so you will need to plan for all these. It is also essential to provide activities both indoors and in the garden, each giving an added dimension to the simple resources you offer.

The messy experiences in this book encourage development and learning through sensory play. They all use sight, touch and smell, and of course, many babies and children will want to taste the experience as well! Enhancing experiences in different ways will expand the use of all senses, for example, by adding food essences, flavours, colours and sounds. Many sensory experiences are enhanced by offering them out of doors, and some children actually learn better in a garden. Apart from being more enjoyable, outside activities are often easier to clear up. (Outdoor provision also recognise the restrictions some settings have on the protection of floors and surfaces in buildings which have shared use or belong to someone else!).

Involving children in the preparation and clearing up of these activities is also part of the learning. Even very young children can help with simple preparation tasks, and as they become more confident and independent, they can begin to make their own dough, mix their own coloured water, select their own materials and resources. Planning and preparing for the activity is often as enjoyable as playing with what you have prepared - and of course, if children help with preparation, they also know where to put the things when they have finished with them.

Your planning of the experiences in this book will take account of your observations of children's play and current interests, their current stage of development (not just their age) and the need to offer a wide range of sensory experiences over the child's time with you. These progressions will help you to plan an appropriate range of experiences, and by suggesting additions and new stimuli as children's needs and abilities develop, you can ensure that the activities are fresh and exciting each time you offer them.

Sally Featherstone, Liz Williams; 2006

Young babies (0-8 months)	Babies (8-18 months)	Young children (18-24 months)	Children (24-36 months)	Foundation 1&2 (3 to 5)

Heads Up, Lookers and Communicators	Sitters, Standers and Explorers	Movers, Shakers and Players	Walkers, Talkers and Pretenders	Moving on into the Foundation Stage

Instant or Whipped Cream or Shaving Foam

These substances all give good sensory experiences, and allow babies and young children to explore using a range of senses. Cream also offers opportunities to taste as well as touch and smell. Cream and aerosol shaving foam have similar but not identical textures.
Choose non-allergenic shaving foams.

Young babies (0-8 months)

Spoon or pour your chosen foam into small trays on the floor at a young baby's level so they can explore it with their hands and fingers, helped by an adult if needed.
Put blobs on small mirrors for exploration. As cream/foam is moved on the surface by a young baby or adult, they will see patterns and reflections. Try putting foams in a builder's tray or 'Tuff spot' for lying in as a sensory experience for the whole body.

Heads Up, Lookers and Communicators

Babies (8-18 months)

Put foam in a variety of shallow containers so babies can trail their fingers through it, repeating and practising making patterns.
Use large trays for sitting or standing in, to explore in more ways. Begin to share the language of texture, rewarding sounds and body movements. Spread foam all over see-through surfaces - windows or perspex sheets. By making patterns on these surfaces, children can reveal what is on the other side – people or objects.

Sitters, Standers and Explorers

Young children (18-24 months)

Add things to cream or foam. Start with food colouring or paint, so children can begin to experience changes. Put some colouring next to the foam so children can incorporate it themselves. Use foams on different surfaces for young children to experiment how it feels. Make 'pictures' on different papers, plastic, wood, paving, glass, mirror, bubble wrap, card. Encourage the children to talk about what they are doing, feeling, finding out.

Movers, Shakers and Players

Children (24-36 months)

Place foams in deeper trays and create a treasure hunt for children by hiding buttons, pebbles, coins, big beads, small world figures etc. Develop texture by adding glitter, pasta, lentils, sand, beads etc. Children can begin to make their own patterns in the foam or cream, developing wrist, finger and hand control, mark-making skills and hand-eye co-ordination. Try foams on flat sheets of card, plastic or a cheap shower curtain.

Walkers, Talkers and Pretenders

Foundation 1&2 (3 to 5)

Use coloured foams to develop story telling skills. Add small world, cars, play people, animals, dinosaurs etc. Try using both sides of a perspex sheet to copy patterns or make backgrounds.
Add colours (paint or food colouring) to explore colour mixing or changing. Make repeating patterns, letter shapes, zigzags, loops, circles. Take prints of coloured foam (not cream!) by pressing paper very gently on the pattern and peeling off.

Moving on into the Foundation Stage

Cornflour 'Gloop'

Make gloop by mixing cornflour and water together. This creates a substance unlike any other! Gloop almost appears to have magical qualities. It can be picked up like a solid but tips and pours like a liquid. This is messy, so remove any clothing that could suffer, or protect the children!

Young babies (0-8 months)

Place gloop in small trays at floor level. Encourage the young baby to watch an adult playing with the gloop and then help the young baby to explore the gloop using hands and fingers.

You could tip the tray so the gloop is a bit deeper and easier to pick up. Some babies may need a bit of encouragement to get their fingers in this mixture. Take your time, be patient and encouraging.

Heads Up, Lookers and Communicators

Babies (8-18 months)

Put the gloop in large accessible trays and encourage the babies to play with it. They will enjoy just touching it, picking it up and moving it round, and letting it drizzle through their fingers. Babies could also sit or stand in the gloop and feel the texture with feet, legs and other parts of their bodies. You could remove clothes and let them experience the gloop in just a nappy. Talk with them about the mixture and what they are doing.

Sitters, Standers and Explorers

Young children (18-24 months)

Young children can make gloop themselves, investigating the ingredients and properties of dry cornflour before adding water. Encourage the young children to mix the two ingredients together and see what happens – be prepared for both watery and very stiff gloop! Young children may particularly enjoy making patterns in the gloop and just watching them disappear. Add some food colouring for a different experience.

Movers, Shakers and Players

Children (24-36 months)

 Put the gloop at an accessible height and begin to use tools in it - spoons, scrapers, forks, sand rakes, funnels etc.

The children could make gloop by themselves and experiment with adding colours and scents to it, using food colouring, paint or perfumed oils. Talk with them as they work, modelling and encouraging descriptive language as they pick the gloop up, pour it and watch how it changes.

Walkers, Talkers and Pretenders

Foundation 1&2 (3 to 5)

Talk with the children as they explore the gloop, using words like solid and liquid and how gloop appears to be both. Compare gloop with custard powder, cocoa powder and drinking chocolate when they are mixed with water. Try mixing these with other liquids to see what happens. Removing drips and drops from surfaces has its own fascination - offer the children scrapers or old credit or loyalty cards for clearing up time, and they will love it!

Moving on into the Foundation Stage

Dough

There are many types of dough which can be safely used with babies and children. Dough is a holistic learning experience for babies and young children, meeting both emotional and physical needs. Dough needs to be experienced for its own properties before adding tools for modelling.

See The Little Book of Dough for lots of dough recipes.

Young babies (0-8 months)

Use soft, very pliable dough with young babies. This will allow them to touch it, squeeze it, poke it and make it move through their fingers. Sensory experience will be increased if you add colourings, perfumes or safe textures.

Try: orange, lemon or vanilla flavouring;
aromatherapy oils;
food colourings;
porridge oats, rice grains, pasta stars.

Heads Up, Lookers and Communicators

Babies (8-18 months)

 Make big quantities of dough so babies can explore it by sitting and standing in it. Colour and perfume the dough sometimes. Children will be able to experiment by squeezing the dough with different parts of their body, and making imprints in it with fingers, hands, toes etc. Encourage them to start using individual fingers, palms and sides of their hands, by playing alongside with your own hands. Don't force them if they just want to squeeze!

Sitters, Standers and Explorers

Young children (18-24 months)

Encourage young children to model the dough by using their hands, fingers, thumbs, wrists, palms, sides of their palms. Let them explore patting and rolling it into shapes with their hands.

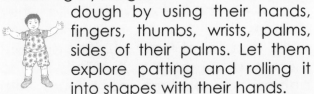

As young children begin to develop their fine motor skill they can start to use simple tools to explore the dough: sticks, smooth and textured rolling pins, stones, nail brushes, toothbrushes etc. Encourage and praise the experience, not the product!

Movers, Shakers and Players

Children (24-36 months)

With adult help, children can begin to mix their own dough. Add glitter, pasta or colourings to dough recipes. Begin to offer a variety of tools such as plastic scissors, sieves, combs, sticks. Introduce cutters. Children can now use the dough to add to their role play - 'baking' cakes or pizzas in the home corner, or making salt dough decorations for the garden. As the children talk about what they are doing, dough play will help extend their vocabulary.

Walkers, Talkers and Pretenders

Foundation 1&2 (3 to 5)

Using a variety of simple recipes, children can make a variety of doughs completely independently. They will be able to talk about the differences between doughs, some are stretchy, some stiff, some watery, some last longer, some go hard. Adding colouring with the liquid or kneading it in later, or adding texture and perfume can enhance the experience. Try some doughs that bake hard, and make role play props or models for small world play.

Moving on into the Foundation Stage

Bubbles

Bubbles are great for helping babies and young children to practice and perfect following with their eyes. Try bubbles of different types, and use simple tools to make bubbles in liquids. This develops physical and fine motor control. Add glycerine or a bit of sugar to make bubbles last longer

Be aware of allergies when choosing bubble mixtures.

Young babies (0-8 months)

Babies love bubbles, and for many it is a real treat which will continue to fascinate them for increasing lengths of time as they grow. Blow bubbles near babies for them to follow with their eyes - blow them above, on a level, from behind the baby to develop anticipation, focus and eye movement. Make sure some bubbles land on their hands, feet or arms so they can feel the sensation of the bubbles popping on their skin.

Heads Up, Lookers and Communicators

Babies (8-18 months)

Blow bubbles near bright lights so babies can watch the colours reflected in their surfaces.

Whisk up piles of foam bubbles and put them in a 'tuff spot' or builder's tray so babies can explore the texture with hands, feet, bodies. Add some paint for coloured bubbles. Try a bubble machine for a very calming experience for babies and adults.

Be alert - bubbles make surfaces and babies very slippery!

Sitters, Standers and Explorers

Young children (18-24 months)

Use bubble bath, soap flakes, gentle shampoo or foaming bubbles to make different sorts and textures of bubbles. Put them in large or small trays for young children to explore. Encourage the children to explore the bubbles with tools such as whisks and forks to develop their fine motor skills as they make different sized bubbles. Blow bubbles out of doors on a windy day. Make home made bubble blowers from soft wire.

Movers, Shakers and Players

Children (24-36 months)

Encourage young children to chase, catch and pop bubbles blown both indoors and in the garden.
The experience will vary depending on the weather and the bubble liquid used. Talk to the children about how it feels to catch and pop a bubble. Put a bubble machine just inside an open window, so the bubbles fly out of the window and across the garden. Watch, chase and pop the bubbles as they fly.

Walkers, Talkers and Pretenders

Foundation 1&2 (3 to 5)

Help the children to blow their own bubbles using a range of tools - wands, string bubble makers, multi-hole bubble blowers, straws, pipes etc. Let children experiment and decide what makes the best bubbles - washing up liquid, soap flakes, etc. Catch a bubble in a bubble wand and try to blow more from it. Which tools make the best bubbles? Look for bubbles in carbonated drinks, in water from a fast tap, bubble wrap or speech bubbles in comics.

Moving on into the Foundation Stage

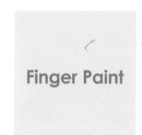

Finger Paint

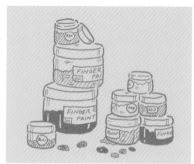

Check to be sure that the paint is suitable for young children and use one of the wide range of finger paints specially produced for children. Watch to see which they like best, try different colours, textures and thicknesses. You could make your own finger paint by mixing paint and moisturiser (this stops paint staining hands and other skin areas!).

Young babies (0-8 months)

Encourage young babies to feel paint by touching and lying in it - protect their clothes or strip them down to a nappy. You can put the paint in shallow containers on the floor, on the tray of a high chair, or just in a puddle near where they are lying or sitting.

Clear or reflective surfaces such as plastic sheet, acrylic, a mirror or a window can attract young babies to this activity.

Heads Up, Lookers and Communicators

Babies (8-18 months)

Babies can be encouraged to investigate paint by smearing it on a range of equipment such as plates, boards, mirrors, paper, glass, fabric or tiles. Try sitting a baby in the middle of a big piece of paper or card so they can paint all round themselves. If they are interested in tools, start offering brushes, dabbers, sponges or other mark makers. Try using finger paint to cover plastic animals, dinosaurs or dolls from the home corner!

Sitters, Standers and Explorers

Young children (18-24 months)

As young children begin to develop their physical skills let them use hands and feet to make marks on paper or on outdoor surfaces. Encourage them to talk about what is happening with the marks or colours. Offer access to a wide variety of brushes and rollers, and encourage young children to use water and paint on a range of surfaces and at different heights. These could include fences, paving slabs, paper on easels and tables.

Movers, Shakers and Players

Children (24-36 months)

Encourage children to investigate painting with hands, fingers and feet, developing more controlled movements. This could include making footprints and hand-prints. Enhance paint by adding glitter, washing up liquid (bubbles), sand, sawdust or paste, for different experiences. Use paint to redecorate your home corner or climbing fame. Make a huge finger painting on a wall, a path or a sheet in the garden and hose it off again.

Walkers, Talkers and Pretenders

Foundation 1&2 (3 to 5)

Encourage paint mixing, and offer children a choice of materials to make their own textured paint. Discuss with the children the advantages and disadvantages of thick and thin paint, and different textures. Try hand sprayers on a shower curtain outside. Offer children other tools to use for paint and print - kitchen tools are great.

Keep on encouraging the use of fingers, hands (and feet) for both painting and printing.

Moving on into the Foundation Stage

Compost

Older children will love compost as a new and different medium for their play.

Be specially careful when using compost with babies - buy new compost and make sure you supervise the experience at all times, so the babies don't eat too much!

Young babies (0-8 months)

Let babies feel the texture of dry compost as it is sprinkled on their hands, feet and bodies. Hold them upright and let them 'walk' on it or hold them so they can reach out to feel the texture with their hands and fingers.

Take a soft toy, a teddy or other animal for a walk in the compost tray.

Heads Up, Lookers and Communicators

Babies (8-18 months)

Mix the compost with other safe gardening materials – sand, gravel etc and let babies explore the different textures. Lift babies so they can feel the compost on the soles of their bare feet. Let standers and explorers walk in shallow trays of compost and sand mixture. Hide objects in the compost for them to find. Alter the texture by adding water, making a path of smooth pebbles, dropping some glitter, adding small shells or sequins.

Sitters, Standers and Explorers

Young children (18-24 months)

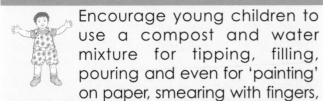

Encourage young children to use a compost and water mixture for tipping, filling, pouring and even for 'painting' on paper, smearing with fingers, hands, feet, or making body prints out of doors in a large space. Remember that it is the process which is important, end products are an extra and of less interest to most children at this stage.
Walking or riding through piles of compost is another popular game!

Movers, Shakers and Players

Children (24-36 months)

Encourage children to mix compost with other substances in different size containers, and then explore it with tools – dig, build, spread, sieve, etc – dry and wet. Try sand, gravel, leaves, beads, Perlite. Talk with the children about what they are doing, seeing and discovering. Play 'hide and find' with small world people and animals or natural objects such as polished stones, shells, driftwood, glass beads, nuts and acorns.

Walkers, Talkers and Pretenders

Foundation 1&2 (3 to 5)

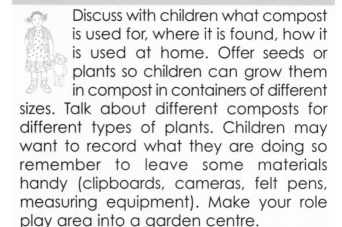

Discuss with children what compost is used for, where it is found, how it is used at home. Offer seeds or plants so children can grow them in compost in containers of different sizes. Talk about different composts for different types of plants. Children may want to record what they are doing so remember to leave some materials handy (clipboards, cameras, felt pens, measuring equipment). Make your role play area into a garden centre.

Moving on into the Foundation Stage

Sand

Sand is the most familiar, but can also be the most neglected activity! It can be used in many different ways for children of all ages, and they love it. It is one material they may have had some experience of at home. Remember that some children don't like materials that stick to their hands, so offer both wet and dry sand.

Use fine silver sand for small children, the younger the child, the finer and cleaner the sand needs to be. Make sure babies can reach the sand from their position on the floor or on your lap.

Put some dry sand in a shallow tray such as a plant saucer, and encourage them to trail their hands in it, or try wet sand to poke and squeeze. Babies need close supervision when playing with sand - it isn't dangerous to eat, but needs a watchful eye.

Heads Up, Lookers and Communicators

Make sure babies can get into sand containers to sit, crawl and lie in the sand. Have an outdoor 'crawl-in' sand pit. Help the babies to pour or scoop dry sand over their legs, arms and bodies. Let them squeeze it between their fingers and rub it on their skin. Talk with them about what they are doing as they do it. Praise their sounds and words.

Model words, movements and activities if they need some help.

Sitters, Standers and Explorers

Young children (18-24 months)

Let young children explore sand with simple tools of an appropriate size (spades, sieves, bowls, scoops, funnels, containers). They may begin to transfer sand between containers or transport it around outside. They will begin to mould it with their hands if it is wet. Put damp sand in shallow trays and leave some toy cars or animals to make tracks and prints. Offer patty pans, or sand moulds for more damp sand creativity.

Movers, Shakers and Players

Children (24-36 months)

Offer substances and small objects for the children to mix with the sand and use creatively - glitter, sequins, shells, glue, pasta, dough, paint. Discuss with the children what they are doing, how it feels and what it looks like. Explore how the sand changes when mixed with other things. Encourage children to use sand in role-play by adding small world toys. Talk with the children about what is happening, developing their play.

Walkers, Talkers and Pretenders

Foundation 1&2 (3 to 5)

Extend and continue all the suggested ways of using sand. Children need to revisit activities and experiences so they can make sense of what they learn. Expand the experience by exploring coloured sand, sand of different grades. Discuss where sand comes from, how it is used in building and construction, creatures that live in the sand, deserts, beaches. Make a desert or beach in small world play. Draw and make marks in wet sand.

Moving on into the Foundation Stage

21

Soap flakes

Soap flakes are worth looking for - they are not easy to find, but demand is bringing them back! Don't use detergent instead. Mix some soap flakes with warm water in a bowl or other container. Leave the mixture to stand until it becomes thick, adding more water if it needs it. The mixture will be slimy and slidey. It's called Slime!

Young babies (0-8 months)

Spoon or pour into small trays on the floor at a young baby's level so they can explore it with their hands and fingers, helped by an adult if needed.

Put blobs on small mirrors for exploration. As the slime is moved on the surface by a young baby or adult, the baby will see patterns and reflections.

Or put in a builders' tray or 'Tuff spot' for lying in as a whole body experience. Take care about eyes!

Heads Up, Lookers and Communicators

Babies (8-18 months)

Use in large trays for sitting or standing in. Place in a variety of shallow containers so babies can trail their fingers through, lifting the Slime in the air and letting it drip between their fingers. Talk about the feel and movement of the stuff, watching for body movements and sounds of enjoyment.

Put some on see-through surfaces such as windows, mirrors or perspex sheets. Add some food colouring for a change.

Sitters, Standers and Explorers

Young children (18-24 months)

Continue to add things to Slime - food colouring, paint, sequins, little beads or small pasta shapes so the children can begin to experience changes.

Use Slime on different surfaces, to make smeary patterns, for use with card combs, funnels, spoons and cups, to pour and mix and drizzle. Encourage young children to talk about what they are doing, feeling and finding out.

Movers, Shakers and Players

Children (24-36 months)

Let the children help you to mix the Slime, then give them whisks, beaters or forks to beat it into foam. Add other kitchen gadgets to explore the Slime with. You could make a really big quantity of Slime and put it outside in a paddling pool so children can sit in it. Take care and stay close, it's slippy! Or you could put Slime in a bowl on the floor and let children put their feet in it to see how that feels. Put the bowl on a towel.

Walkers, Talkers and Pretenders

Foundation 1&2 (3 to 5)

Give the children the ingredients and a simple pictorial recipe and let them make their own Slime, colouring it as they wish - black or green will probably be favourites! Talk with them as they make the Slime and play with it, exploring the process of mixing, whisking, colouring, as well as how the Slime feels as they work. Give them a really big bowl - can they make the Slime fill the bowl? What makes the Slime get bigger?

Moving on into the Foundation Stage

Ketchup, Jelly and Custard

Some food substances offer very good messy experiences, but check with your managers before using food items for play. Ketchup, jelly and custard are all familiar, cheap and safe to use even with very small children. The ideas here can be used for any of the three.

Young babies (0-8 months)

Jelly is a good substance for early sensory learning.
Its texture can range between liquid and various stages of setting.
In addition it can offer a range of colours, flavours and scents. Make jelly in small moulds, bowls or cups and tip out onto plastic plates for babies to look at, smell, feel and taste. You can put jelly on chair trays, near the baby on the floor or on a low table as you sit close, with the baby on your knee or in your lap.

Heads Up, Lookers and Communicators

Babies (8-18 months)

Ketchup on a shallow tray will provide an absorbing activity for fingers and hands, and is very good for helping babies to isolate one finger. It will also help them to find their mouth as they taste the ketchup.
Try putting small pieces of soft fruit such as banana in custard to encourage babies to feed themselves with their fingers. Set small pieces of fruit in small jellies for exploration and grasping practice.

Sitters, Standers and Explorers

Young children (18-24 months)

Offer custard and jelly at snack time, and encourage young children to help themselves. It is easier if the jelly is broken up a bit with a fork before they try to spoon it. Offering ketchup or plain yogurt with vegetable sticks makes a good snack alternative as well as helping children to improve their fine motor control. Squeezing ketchup from plastic bottles helps hand muscles to develop. Try adding cornfour to boiling water (adult only preparation!) for tactile play.

Movers, Shakers and Players

Children (24-36 months)

Make big quantities of jelly in a water tray - leave to set over night and see how the children play with it in the morning! Don't be in a hurry to give them tools. Just let them use their hands and fingers.

Let the children help you make custard - mixing custard powder with water and watching what happens when you add the hot milk. Then let the children cut banana slices for banana custard.

Walkers, Talkers and Pretenders

Foundation 1&2 (3 to 5)

Make a water tray full of green or blue jelly and set some small world sea creatures in it. When the jelly is set, let the children find the creatures. Try setting spiders in blackcurrant jelly or bugs in green jelly so children can discover them. Use squeezy ketchup bottles and plastic tomatoes to make patterns on paper, plastic trays or home made pizza bases. Make low sugar custard for snack - some children who won't drink milk will eat custard !

Moving on into the Foundation Stage

Cooked Pasta

Cooked pasta of all sorts is ideal for developing hand and finger control - it's also great fun for children of all ages. Try to find different sorts (tubes, spaghetti, noodles, stars, sheets, animal shapes). Cook the pasta in boiling water till it is 'al dente' and let it cool before using. <u>Add a bit of oil to stop the pasta sticking together.</u>

Young babies (0-8 months)

Noodles are a quick and easy baby play material as they only need boiling water (cool them under a cold tap before using). Offer young babies a couple of strands of spaghetti or noodles to hold and feel in their fingers. Stay with them and talk as they play. Put a shallow bowl of cooked pasta near a lying baby and let them reach for the sensation. You could also put some cooked pasta on the tray of a high chair or a table top.

Heads Up, Lookers and Communicators

Babies (8-18 months)

Babies will enjoy having some small pasta shapes to pick up. They could put them in a bowl, or post them in a tube if they don't want to eat them! This helps with pincer grip and hand control.
Cooked spaghetti, coloured with food colouring makes a new experience, offer small quantities to individuals, so they have their own bowl or dish.

Sitters, Standers and Explorers

Young children (18-24 months)

Make large quantities of cooked spaghetti or other types of pasta, adding colouring to the cooking water if you wish. Try orange, red or black food colouring paste for a strong colour. Put the pasta in a deep bowl or water tray so several children can explore it together.
You can also use cooked pasta to make pictures without glue - drizzle or arrange shapes and strands on paper and they will stick with their own starch.

Movers, Shakers and Players

Children (24-36 months)

Add small world creatures to cooked pasta for small world play. Try making blue spaghetti, putting it in a paddling pool and adding sea creatures.
Offer some kitchen tools and saucepans for pretend play and developing hand control - try strainers, tongs, spoons, tweezers, pasta lifters.
Add spaghetti to a water tray and watch what happens as the pasta dissolves in the water.

Walkers, Talkers and Pretenders

Foundation 1&2 (3 to 5)

Offer cooked pasta outside to make patterns, shapes and scenes on paving stones and paths. Leave the remains for the birds to eat.
Offer the children different colours of food colouring to make their own coloured pasta - put some cooked pasta and chosen colouring in a zip lock plastic bag and children can squidge it about with their hands until it is coloured. Use for free play, pictures or role play.

Moving on into the Foundation Stage

Clay

Clay is a natural material and is a wonderful play experience for children of all ages. Don't worry about 'finished results' the experience is the thing! Buy clay from reputable suppliers where it has been cleaned and stones have been removed. Make sure the clay is moist enough for the children to manipulate, and store under a wet cloth between sessions.

Young babies (0-8 months)

Use white or grey clay with babies as it doesn't stain like red clay. Offer a lump to poke and squeeze, holding it in your hand where the baby can see it and can see your response to their experiments. Talk to them as they explore, encouraging movements and new experiences, (if they do eat some, it won't be much if you are there to watch). Mix some clay with water to a liquid state for smearing on surfaces, trays, mirrors etc.

Heads Up, Lookers and Communicators

Babies (8-18 months)

Put some clay in flat trays such as builder's trays for babies to explore with their whole bodies. If the clay is soft, they will experiment with smearing it on their hands, arms and legs. Encourage babies to use clay standing at a low table, where they can pat, squeeze and shape it, strengthening their hands and fingers and improving their balance as they play. Sit with them, but try to avoid instructing them - just let them experience what they can do.

Sitters, Standers and Explorers

Young children (18-24 months)

At this age, young children will begin to experiment with rolling, shaping and 'making sausages'. Watch for this and encourage their experiments by copying in the play. Rolling pins and patty pans may be offered at this stage, because children may want to organise the shapes they make. Intervene sensitively and don't go too fast, and don't be upset if they ignore the things you offer - they will come to them later.

Movers, Shakers and Players

Children (24-36 months)

This is the stage when children make representations of the things they see, so they will probably respond to having a basket or box of tools and shapers for the clay. They will also enjoy using different colours and types of clay. Offer small rolling pins, cutters, bun trays, paper bun cases, blunt knives, textured rollers etc. They may also begin to want to keep some of the things they have made, or to use them in role play or with small world.

Walkers, Talkers and Pretenders

Foundation 1&2 (3 to 5)

You could buy clay mixed with nylon strands, which hardens without a kiln. Children will love using this to make and paint their own plates, bowls, and objects for pretend play. You could also show them how to make decorative plaques from flat pieces of clay, pressing tools and objects into the surface (natural objects and tools). Older children can begin to relate the clay they play with to finished articles of pottery, plates, mugs or ornaments, and discuss changes.

Moving on into the Foundation Stage

Steam

Steam and condensation are fascinating and free resources, but we often forget that for children they can be even more magical, specially because they appear and disappear without warning! Find ways for using this free resource with babies and children.

Be careful with very hot water - steam can burn!

Young babies (0-8 months)

Hold babies so they can pat and smear their hands and fingers in steam on windows and mirrors. Sit in a chair with a safe baby mirror and explore the way your breath hides their picture. Make sure you have mirrors in your changing rooms or by your changing tables, so you can experiment together at changing time.

Encourage parents to explore steamy mirrors and windows with their babies at home.

Heads Up, Lookers and Communicators

Babies (8-18 months)

Breathe gently on a mirror or window and help them to reveal themselves in it by removing the steam. Take little opportunities at changing time to draw, scribble and otherwise explore steam on mirrors etc. Encourage babies to separate their index fingers when drawing on windows.

Talk about bathrooms and bath times. Encourage parents to use this free mark making opportunity at bath time.

Sitters, Standers and Explorers

Young children (18-24 months)

Make hand prints on steamy windows. Drive toy cars to make tracks in the steam. Use sponges to clean the windows on a steamy day.

Talk about the steam rising from warm water as they wash their hands. Fill a water tray outside with warm water (big quantities of water will keep their heat for a longer time) and talk about the steam - where does it come from, what is it?

Movers, Shakers and Players

Children (24-36 months)

Offer children window scrapers and sponges to use on condensation on windows. This sometimes forms outdoors and sometimes indoors - watch for the opportunities and catch the moment - this is an activity that can't be planned! You can also use the scrapers on rainy or frosty days outside to clean rain and ice from windows and other surfaces. Look to see if the pattern is still there next time the window steams up.

Walkers, Talkers and Pretenders

Foundation 1&2 (3 to 5)

Older children will be able to spot steam from kettles, pans, tumble driers - as long as you keep them at a safe distance. Take the opportunity to explore their 'steamy' breath on cold days and the steam that rises from warm water if you take it outside. Talk about why this happens outside and not inside. In a warm bathroom, try just cleaning their own face shape from a steamy mirror and then adding curly hair round it in the steam. Or make secret peep holes in steamy windows to peep out at the world.

Moving on into the Foundation Stage

31

Ice

Ice is another fascinating substance to explore. It is virtually free and very easy to make.

If children are playing with ice for any length of time, make sure they don't get too cold, and offer gloves if they play outside.

Try exploring the sound and sight of ice cubes in a drink. Put water or dilute squash in a clear plastic cup or bottle and add some ice cubes. Let the baby watch the ice cubes as they swish in the drink; let them touch the cold container. Talk to them about what you can see, and hold out an ice cube on your hand for them to touch, hold or taste. Try putting a zip lock bag of coloured ice cubes near where a baby is lying, for them to touch and pat.

Heads Up, Lookers and Communicators

Make some ice cubes with objects frozen inside - pasta shapes, flowers, leaves, raisins. Offer a few in a bowl and see what happens. Float clear ice cubes in containers of water or tip a few into a shallow tray where the baby can reach them from a sitting or crawling position. Encourage the babies to try touching different parts of their bodies

with ice cubes to feel the ice on their skins, and see how it melts with the warmth.

Sitters, Standers and Explorers

Young children (18-24 months)

Why not buy a bag of ice from a supermarket and tip it into a builder's tray or water tray. Children could explore the ice with boots on or with their hands (with or without gloves). You could tip cubes into sand or water, foam or Gloop and see what happens as the children play. Add some food colouring to water and freeze cubes of different colours to float in water or play with in containers, or to add to drinks at snack time.

Movers, Shakers and Players

Children (24-36 months)

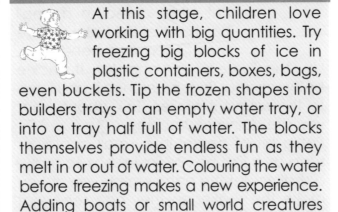 At this stage, children love working with big quantities. Try freezing big blocks of ice in plastic containers, boxes, bags, even buckets. Tip the frozen shapes into builders trays or an empty water tray, or into a tray half full of water. The blocks themselves provide endless fun as they melt in or out of water. Colouring the water before freezing makes a new experience. Adding boats or small world creatures extends imaginative play.

Walkers, Talkers and Pretenders

Foundation 1&2 (3 to 5)

Children could make their own ice cubes by filling trays or ice cube bags with plain or coloured water, adding things like sequins, little beads, flower, buttons etc. These can be floated in water or played with on their own. Extend their imaginations by suggesting some unusual ice moulds such as rubber gloves, wellies, plastic bags, jelly moulds, egg boxes etc. Try some experiments with melting (eg sprinkle salt on ice), or colouring (adding different sorts of paint).

Moving on into the Foundation Stage

Cornflakes and other cereals

Small or large quantities of dry cereals are good for creative play. Ask parents or your local shop to donate 'past the sell-by date' packs or ends of packets to avoid the sensitivity of using food for play. The added benefits of this play are that if children do eat a bit of it they will come to no harm, and the birds can eat the left overs!

Young babies (0-8 months)

 Put some cereal in a small bowl and let the baby dangle their fingers and hands in it. Lift the cereal up and let it trickle between your fingers, scrunch it and listen to the sound it makes. Talk about what you are doing as you play.

Put a bit of cereal in a small container such as a film box or similar box to make a shaker - let the baby watch you as you make the shaker, so they can see what goes in.

Heads Up, Lookers and Communicators

Babies (8-18 months)

Put cereals on different surfaces such as tin trays, plastic sheeting, fabric and listen to the different sounds. Pour a pack on a builder's tray and let the children stomp on it (with bare feet if possible).

Let standing babies play with mixtures of cereals (adding rice or dry pasta shapes) in bowls or water trays.

Give them containers so they can pour and scoop the dry cereal in and out of bowls and cups.

Sitters, Standers and Explorers

Young children (18-24 months)

Offer some cereals with spoons, scoops and bowls for pretend play. Add wide mouthed funnels and jugs for pouring to strengthen wrist and hand actions. Let them squeeze and squash the cereals in their hands and fingers. Talk about the sound and feel of the different cereals as they handle them. Get a box of Cheerios and see how they stick on young skin - on fingers, faces, arms and legs. Try balancing one on each finger of each hand!

Movers, Shakers and Players

Children (24-36 months)

Put some small paper or plastic bags and scoops out with the dry cereals and encourage fine motor skills in pouring and filling the bags.

Hide small world creatures such as bugs and insects in the cereals for the children to find. By this stage, children will not be so likely to eat play items, so you could add other foods to the mixture - dried beans, peas, rice, very small pasta shapes, seeds.

Walkers, Talkers and Pretenders

Foundation 1&2 (3 to 5)

Offer the different cereals (and rice, beans, pasta etc) in separate bowls or containers with scoops, spoons, plastic cups, ladles, bags and boxes. You could even add a pair of balance scales (no weights). Don't suggest what they should play, just see what happens. Inevitably the different materials will get mixed up during play, so another challenge is to talk about how you could sort them out again!

Moving on into the Foundation Stage

35

Sugar and sugar water

There are many different sorts of sugar - icing, caster, granulated, demerara, soft brown - even coffee sugar crystals and sugar cubes - experiment with them all.

Even the granulated sugars dissolve fairly quickly in water, so play with them dry some-times too, or offer water as a second or alter-native part of the play.

Young babies (0-8 months)

Let young babies feel and touch different dry sugars as well as sugar and water mixtures. Let them watch you mix some icing and see how it behaves as you pour it from a spoon.

Sugar cubes are also fun to hold and then watch them dissolve in a small saucer of water - disappearing as you watch.

Heads Up, Lookers and Communicators

Babies (8-18 months)

Offer different sugars in shallow trays for children to feel and explore. Mix sugars with water and add a small amount of food colouring. Use this mixture to spread on flat surfaces or card, plastic or mirrors. Or make finger paint with 1/3 cup cornfour, 3 tbsp sugar and 2 cups cold water. Add food colouring and offer for painting on card, paper, tabletops or even windows! Use this mixture outside on a fence or wall - a hose will wash it off.

Sitters, Standers and Explorers

Young children (18-24 months)

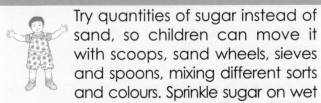 Try quantities of sugar instead of sand, so children can move it with scoops, sand wheels, sieves and spoons, mixing different sorts and colours. Sprinkle sugar on wet or glued paper to make patterns - a mixture of sugar and powder paint sprinkled onto wet paper makes lovely patterns. Soak sticks of chalk in sugar and water mix for five to ten minutes - this makes the colours MUCH brighter, and stops the chalk smudging so much.

Movers, Shakers and Players

Children (24-36 months)

Help the children to make their own coloured icings and drizzle them on biscuits (bought or home made). Help the children to paint sheets of paper with a mixture of 5tsp sugar with 25ml water. Drop paint from straws, droppers or brushes while the paper is still wet and watch what happens. The painty sugar mixture makes wonderful patterns that spread as you look. Use two or three colours for best effect.

Walkers, Talkers and Pretenders

Foundation 1&2 (3 to 5)

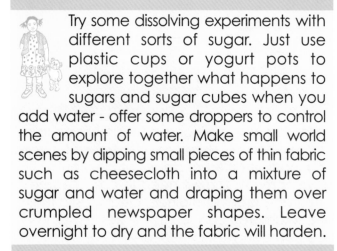 Try some dissolving experiments with different sorts of sugar. Just use plastic cups or yogurt pots to explore together what happens to sugars and sugar cubes when you add water - offer some droppers to control the amount of water. Make small world scenes by dipping small pieces of thin fabric such as cheesecloth into a mixture of sugar and water and draping them over crumpled newspaper shapes. Leave overnight to dry and the fabric will harden.

Moving on into the Foundation Stage

Coloured Water

Colouring water brings a new dimension to a simple resource. Here are a few ideas for ways of using ti at different stages of children's development. You will need to collect some safe transparent containers, clear plastic tubing etc, so children can see the water travelling as well as moving it themselves.

Try www.commotiongroup.co.uk for pipettes, funnels, clear tubing and plastic test tubes.

Young babies (0-8 months)

Put different coloured water in small jars (such as baby food jars) so babies can touch them and see the water moving. Leave coloured water jars on a window sill near quiet areas, changing tables or cots so the sun can shine through them. Or hang plastic test tubes of coloured water up to make a mobile, adding some CDs and mirror strips.

Heads Up, Lookers and Communicators

Babies (8-18 months)

Half fill <u>tough</u> zip-lock bags with coloured water (you could add a bit of cellulose paste powder to thicken it up a bit). Zip the bags and let babies play with them - squeezing, pummelling, patting and squashing them (if you are worried about the bags splitting, seal the ends with silver duct tape)then they can even walk on the bags! Fill plastic test tubes with different coloured waters. Cap them and stand them in a test tube stand or a bowl of sand.

Sitters, Standers and Explorers

Young children (18-24 months)

Put coloured water in water trays - by adding food colouring. Offer spoons, cups, buckets, water wheels and funnels for play indoors and outside. Try some unusual colours - purple, black, lime green, orange, brown (even periwinkle or heliotrope). Add some thickening some-times - such as jelly or non-fungicidal cellulose paste powder. Mix sequins, leaves, or small beads in the water or goo and offer nets for catching.

Movers, Shakers and Players

Children (24-36 months)

Add some small world figures - animals, sea creatures, bugs, or people to coloured water. Offer sieves, funnels, droppers, clear tubing and safe syringes to the collection of resources for them to select from. Always put the resources in a trolley, box or basket by the water, so children can choose their own things - water trays often get so full of stuff that there is no room to play, so watch and help by removing things they are not using.

Walkers, Talkers and Pretenders

Foundation 1&2 (3 to 5)

Make 'under the sea jars' using screw topped jars. Help them make some bluey-green water. Now help the children to put some sand in the bottom of each jar, add a few shells and carefully fill the jar with blue water. Add some fish and seaweed (cut them from coloured plastic carrier bags) and screw the top on tightly (duct tape will make it really waterproof). The children can experiment with their jars, making waves and storms - watching and talking about what happens.

Moving on into the Foundation Stage

Titles in the Baby and Beyond series will include:

* Marks and Mark Making
* **Stories, Songs and Rhymes**
* Puppets, Soft Toys and Dolls
* Music and Sound
* Cooking
* The Natural World

* Fine motor skills
* **Small World Play**
* Sensory Experiences
* Finger Songs and Rhymes
* Construction
* Bikes, prams and pushchairs